FRANCE

FRANCE

Pierre Brodin

Doubleday & Company, Inc., Garden City, New York
1973

ISBN: 0-385-03300-1 Trade
0-385-05267-7 Prebound
Library of Congress Catalog Card Number 72–92194
Copyright © 1973 by Pierre Brodin

Contents

List of Illustrations

I
A Moderate and Highly Diversified Land

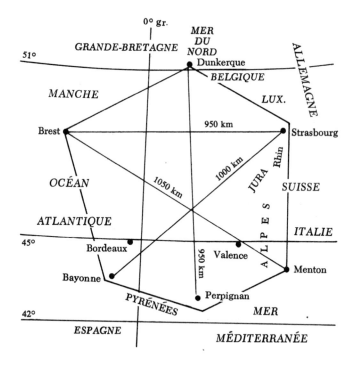

Unlike China, the Soviet Union, or the United States, France is not a land of superlatives and extremes. The French like to say that their country is a temperate, moderate one, scaled down to human needs.

As a matter of fact, France is situated in the Temperate Zone and occupies a privileged position, halfway between the Pole and the Equator, halfway between California and China, between Panama and the Cape of Good Hope. It is both a continental and a maritime country. Facing America, not very distant from Africa, its 1,250 miles of coastline open on the four most traveled seas of the world: the North Sea, the English Channel, the Atlantic Ocean, and the Mediterranean. France may be looked upon as a bridge between the old and the new worlds.

Its territory, which, as every French schoolboy knows, can be inscribed within the frame of a hexagon, has symmetrical, harmonious proportions. Smaller than Alaska or Texas, France, with its 220,000 square miles, is not a big country, but it is not so small as Belgium or Switzerland. It is, indeed, the largest in Europe, with the exception of the U.S.S.R. whose empire is half-Asiatic.

Its land presents a greater variety than most countries

of comparable area. It has mountains as high as the Sierra Nevada, plains which remind us of the Middle West, shores which, in Brittany, resemble those of New England and, in the South, those of the Carolinas. It even has canyons, such as the picturesque *Gorges du Tarn* in the Massif Central; *badlands* and other geological formations add to the general diversity.

The mountains of France are of two kinds: the high ones, which for many centuries rendered communications difficult, are situated at the frontiers; the others, which belong to the broken eroded ranges of Hercynian Europe, are of moderate height and are no obstacle to human and economic relations.

To the first group belong the Pyrénées in the South; the Alps and the Jura, in the Southeast. The Pyrénées are a very massive barrier between France and Spain. They have high peaks, some rising above 11,000 feet, and high passes, deep and narrow valleys. Their shapes have been sculptured by glacier erosion, often with spectacular results: for instance, the *Cirque de Gavarnie* in Hautes-Pyrénées, a glacial "circus" or bowl-shaped formation resembling a Greek theater of great size, has long been a tourist attraction. The western and eastern Pyrénées have one feature in common: they are less high and have more passes than the central Pyrénées; but otherwise, they present highly divergent aspects: the western or Atlantic Pyrénées are humid and offer green landscapes, the Mediterranean Pyrénées are bare and fragmented.

Alpine ranges act as frontiers between France, Italy, and Switzerland. The French Alps have the highest summits of France: among those, Mont Blanc, which rises

Picturesque Gorges du Tarn. *French Embassy*

to nearly 16,000 feet, is the highest mountain in Europe
if, again, one excepts Russia and its Caucasus. Recently,
in a widely acclaimed feat of engineering, French and
Italian workmen met under its imposing mass as they
created one of the longest tunnels in the world, a remarkable road some seven miles long, linking two countries
which the mountains had formerly separated. The northern Alps have many natural resources, especially hydraulic
power which is used for industrial purposes. These regions
are, on the whole, prosperous and well populated, because
of the presence of hydroelectricity and the winter tourist
trade which flocks to the ski resorts. The southern Alps
are barren limestone mountains of lesser altitude, population, and prosperity.

Parallel to the border between France and Switzerland
lies the Jura, disposed in longitudinal bands. It is a limestone range, covered with forests, meadows, and pastures.

The mountains in the North, West, and center of France
are all older and lower and can be crossed easily. They
are the Ardennes, the Vosges, the hills of Brittany, and the
complex Massif Central.

In the East are the Ardennes, a plateau deeply cut by
rivers, principally by the Meuse. This region is not unlike
the Appalachian Mountains. The Vosges present massive
fir-covered summits called *ballons* because of their
rounded domelike appearance.

Brittany, at the extreme west of France, is a small
peninsula with altitudes of a maximum of 1,000 feet. In
the North and South, the granitic plateaus have been
cut by deep valleys. Inner Brittany, or *Arcoat*, is naturally
poor, was long isolated from the rest of France, and con-

Winter skiers in Haute Garonne. *French Embassy*

trasts with the coast, or *Armor*, which has always been more prosperous thanks to the resources of the sea.

The Massif Central is a complex of plateaus, hills, and mountains, some of which are of volcanic origin. The Auvergne province has the greatest number of extinct volcanoes, called *puys*, of which the best known is the

4,500-foot-high Puy de Dôme. There are also numerous
mineral springs and spas such as Vichy and Royat. South
of Auvergne are high, dry, limestone plateaus known as
the *Causses*. Their rock formations are honeycombed by
grottoes and caves which, in prehistoric times, were the
homes of man's cliff-dwelling ancestors. To the southeast,
the Cévennes are wild and were long deserted; the Protes-
tant dissenters found shelter there in the *désert* when, at
the time of Louis XIV, they were persecuted by the state.

One hundred and five miles south of the mainland,
in the Mediterranean Sea, lies Corsica, the "island of
beauty." It is a mountainous country rising to a maximum
height of 6,600 feet, devoid of natural resources, but a
paradise for the tourists.

Two-thirds of the French land is covered by plains
and farmland.

A continuation of the great European northern plains
and the only natural invasion route into France, the
northern part of the country, comprising Flanders, Artois,
and Picardy, is quite flat, rich, and well populated.

Just south of those regions lie the Parisian basin and
the middle Loire valley. The former, comprising the old
provinces of Île de France, Normandy, and Champagne,
presents the physical aspect of a kind of saucer surrounded by concentric saucers, the rims of which are hills
and plateaus, and looks a bit like an ancient Greek theater. The middle Loire valley is the fertile, mild Touraine,
the "garden of France," which has always attracted
princes and commoners in search of a pleasant environ-
ment.

In the Southwest the triangular Aquitaine basin is also

Loire valley, the "garden of France." *Standard Oil, New Jersey*

very flat and dominated by the influence of the Garonne River, which ties in the surrounding regions.

From the Vosges to the Mediterranean, there are a number of small plains, between the mountains, such as Alsace, Burgundy, and Lyonnais. No part of France is isolated from the others. Depressions and valleys cut through the mountains, uniting regions and opening well-traveled roads. The Rhône valley, for instance, prolonged by the Saône and the Seine valleys, opens a way to the Channel and the Rhône-Saône axis leads through the Burgundy gap to the Alsace-Lorraine and Rhine regions.

While the Rhône, whose waters flow through 328 miles

of French land, may be called unruly and terminates in a useless delta, France has half a dozen very useful rivers, especially the Seine, 485 miles long. The 630-mile-long Loire and the 360-mile-long Garonne are only partly navigable, but they empty into large estuaries which allow the construction of deep harbors. All these rivers are connected by canals into a network of inland waterways.

Diversity and, with a few exceptions, moderation are also to be found in the climate. The eastern part of France and the Alps may have cold snowy winters, but Brittany has the mildness and the dampness of Great Britain, whereas the Côte d'Azur, generally speaking, has the sunny and dry climate of the Italian Riviera. The rest of the country has all the nuances of the western European climate: half continental, half oceanic, it is greatly tempered by the influence of the North Atlantic drift current, the Gulf Stream.

The vegetation and fauna of France are, on the whole, those of western Europe. There is no typical tree which could be what the birch is for Russia or the maple for Canada. The visitor to this country, however, is impressed by the majestic chestnut trees that shade the streets of a great many French cities.

Poplars and elms are found throughout the land, while in the Vosges the fir tree predominates, and the Mediterranean South is characterized by citrus and olive trees. The mulberry also grows in that region so that raising silkworms, which feed on mulberry leaves, is still a thriving industry.

A street in an Alsatian village. *French Embassy*

In the South there are fields of lavender and flowers of all varieties which are picked and processed to provide the essences which will be made into perfume. There and in the rest of the country, farmers raise bees and gather honey.

In general, the fauna of France is indistinguishable from that of the neighboring countries. France, however, raises fewer sheep than Britain, fewer pigs than Germany. This is not surprising since the main dish, the most appreciated, in France, has long been beef steak, called in French *"le bifteck,"* usually served with fried potatoes, which the French enjoy more than any vegetable.

For centuries, France has raised horses, not only sturdy work horses, but thoroughbreds, the aristocrats of the racing world. There are national "haras" or stud farms which ensure the quality and training of horses for show, racing, and international competition. Today, France's stock of horses is as good as that of England, if not better.

Wild animals are rarely to be found in the country: the wild boar and other game are preserved mostly for hunting, a sport which, by the way, hundreds of thousands of Frenchmen practice, whether they follow the hounds in a deer or fox hunt, shoot pheasants, or merely try to bag a lonely rabbit.

The seas and rivers provide France with many varieties of fish, among them carp, trout, sardine, sole and turbot, to the delight of millions of French fishermen and generations of gourmets.

Moderation and diversity are also the main features of France's human geography. France has a population density of 240 inhabitants per square mile, which is average for Europe; it is more populated than Eire (100 inhabitants per square mile) or Norway (30), but less so than some European countries, like the Netherlands, (930), or Italy (425).

The men and women of the South are readily recognizable because of their accent and their easygoing manner. The inhabitants of other regions have specific characteristics and even their own languages: Bretons speak a Celtic tongue; Basques an agglutinative non-Indo-European language, unrelated to any other; Alsatians speak a German dialect; Corsicans a form of Italian; Catalans a variety of Spanish.

Immigration from other lands has further complicated the picture and enriched the human family of France. A look at the sports news will readily confirm this. Not long ago, the French football team had a front line composed of Piantoni, Cisowski, Kopa, Ujlaki, and Wisnieski, all of them French.

The short, dark, mustachioed Latin, who foreigners generally consider typical, is in direct contradiction with the facts, for there is no such thing as an average Frenchman. Rather all types of physical features are to be found in France. Within the last few years, it would seem that the population is decidedly taller on the average than in those years when the privations of successive wars may have had a stunting effect. Fair, blue-eyed Frenchmen in Normandy recall their Viking forebears, Bretons often remind one of the Irish or the Welsh; but, throughout the centuries, there has been constant intermarriage among the various regional strains so that there is absolutely no uniformity in any given province. What Americans call "the melting pot" is very much part of the French scene and aside from consciously maintained bits of folklore and regional tradition, all the many divergent elements have been fused into one nation.

II
From Gaul to De Gaulle: The Past of France

France has a long, rich, colorful, and complex past. The French people, as a whole, know and like their history, as well as their great men: according to a recent poll, Napoleon is still the greatest man of all times for 25 per cent of the population; Louis XIV comes only second, Charles de Gaulle third.

The French do not accept their history passively: for them, it is a living past. Newspaper editors frequently compare contemporary politicians to models of the past such as Richelieu, Colbert, or Clemenceau. In a recent editorial, a leading French newspaper, *Le Figaro*, spoke of two traditions, the authoritarian one, going from Charlemagne to Charles de Gaulle; the gentle one, from Louis le Débonnaire to René Coty (the last, charming but neutral, President of the Fourth Republic). Centenaries are celebrated with great solemnity: the bicentenary of Napoleon's birth was hardly over when preparations were being made for the seventh centenary of St. Louis' departure for the Crusades and his death. The French take pride in the glorious periods of their history: they feel that the part played by France in the affairs of the world has often been greater than her demographic, economic, or military strength. On the other hand, they may have been traumatized by some episodes of that past; repeated invasions, revolutions, and monetary devaluations, "hereditary enemies"—first England, then Germany—and colonialism still play a part in their subconscious.

French schoolboys are pleased to learn that two thousand years before the Christian era, cave dwellers lived in such places as the grottoes of Dordogne. Few western European countries can trace their beginning to such a remote past. That is why a good many names like Cro-Magnon, associated with prehistoric man, are French.

Seven or eight centuries before Christ, some Celtic barbarians named Gauls, coming from the North, invaded the land and mixed with the primitive Ligurian and Iberian peoples. Because of its geographical features, France was populated early. The South-North axis in this country, the shortest route between the shores of the Mediterranean and the lands of the North, was used by the Phoenician and Greek traders, then by the Roman conquerors and the traveling merchants of the Middle Ages.

Six or seven centuries before the Christian era, the Greeks had founded on the shores of the Mediterranean Sea commercial cities like Marseilles, where there is still a "Phocéens" Street—pronounced with the local accent as *Phocéengs.* Nice, the best-known Riviera city today, derives its name from Nike, the Athenian goddess of victory.

The Romans entered Gaul to protect those cities: they conquered the southeast of the country and made of it a *Province,* which is now called *Provence.* In the middle of the first century, Julius Caesar's legions fought the German tribes which had invaded Gaul, and the Romans occupied the whole country, after defeating at Alesia the last Gallic resistance led by Vercingetorix, an Arverne tribesman of central Gaul.

Ancient Gaul and its heroes are the improbable subjects of the most popular comic strip extant: Asterix, the chief character, seems particularly attractive to Frenchmen of all ages who have long considered Vercingetorix their first national hero and who are still looking for the site of Alesia and arguing about its precise whereabouts.

The Roman domination lasted five centuries. It ensured peace and a degree of prosperity. The Romans built roads, developed trade, founded cities, erected monuments, many of which are still almost intact and still in use. The Gauls took to speaking *Latin*, which gradually became their own language, and renounced their own Druidic religions to accept first the Roman gods and then Christianity, imported through Rome.

In the fifth century, the great Germanic invasions everywhere destroyed the Roman domination. The leader of a Frankish tribe, Clovis, accepted Christianity and was baptized at Rheims, where, since then, most of the French Kings received their crown in solemn coronation ceremonies. Clovis, therefore, is generally considered the first King of the country which took the name of France. He continues to be an important historical figure and stories and legends have grown up about him: first graders are often told the story of the "vase de Soissons," according to which Clovis ruthlessly punished a soldier who had defied his authority and broken a vase which the King had promised to his friend, the bishop of Rheims, later known as St. Remi.

After the reign of Clovis, anarchy broke out and lasted until the eighth century, when Charles Martel, the founder of a new dynasty called the *Carolingians,* stopped the Arabian invasion of Gaul on a battlefield located between Tours and Poitiers. For this victory, Charles Martel is called in French mythology the savior of Christendom. His son Pépin became King and his grandson Charlemagne re-established for a while the Roman Empire in the West. He was strongly interested in education, brought foreign scholars to France, and established what might well be the first public schools which considered academic potential as the only criterion for admission. Charlemagne is the unofficially canonized patron of schoolchildren who, at the end of January, celebrate a feast they call the "St. Charlemagne."

In 843, Charlemagne's three grandsons divided his immense territories among themselves, putting an end to the Western Empire, and, in the ninth century, the invasion of the Norman pirates once more created anarchy. Carolingian Kings, in their turn, had become powerless. In 987, a new King, Hughes Capet, founded a new dynasty called the *Capetians.*

The first Capetian Kings owned only the region around Paris known as Île de France, but they slowly extended their conquests. They had to fight, however, with the English: after the marriage of Aliénor of Aquitaine and Henry Plantagenet, the English King was more powerful in France than the King of France. Tenaciously, Philippe Auguste fought and recaptured Normandy, Maine, and

Anjou; and in 1214, at Bouvines, defeated the Emperor of Germany, who was the ally of the English, in what is considered the first great national victory won by Frenchmen.

Another very popular King was Louis IX, or St. Louis, who personally cared for the sick and the deprived and administered justice, put an end to the war with the English and took part in two Crusades against the Moslems. He died in 1270, leaving the memory of a generous man and of the most pious, the most deeply human, the most Christian King.

Between 1337 and 1453, western Europe was again devastated by conflicts which came to be known as the Hundred Years' War. Charles VII had kept only a small portion of France, and the King of England seemed to have definitely triumphed, when suddenly appeared in quasi-miraculous fashion a teen-aged girl from Domremy, in Lorraine, Joan of Arc. Joan was convinced of her divine mission to save her country and managed to break down all incredulity and opposition, obtaining from the King the command of the French troops. She led Charles to Rheims, where he was crowned, and aroused the heart and spirit of the people. At the height of her success, she was betrayed into the hands of the English who had her tried by an ecclesiastical court hoping thus to discredit her. Although she was burned at the stake as a witch, the people were convinced of the authenticity of her mission and drove the English once again out of France. Almost immediately, Joan was acclaimed as a national heroine, and she has remained so for believers and unbelievers alike. Much later, she was canonized by the Church and,

Statue of Joan of Arc in Rheims.

as St. Joan, is considered the patron saint of France.

The next memorable episode of French history takes place at the end of the fifteenth century and the beginning of the sixteenth century, when French Kings tried to obtain lands in Italy. These expeditions had few practical results from the military standpoint, but brought the French into contact with a country which was already deeply involved in the *Renaissance*. Italian thought and artistic forms, as well as the revolution brought about by the invention of printing, transformed French civilization. On Gallic territory, however, the Renaissance flowered on specifically Gallic terms.

One of the consequences of the new humanistic fervor and re-examination of basic texts led to evangelism, a return to scriptural writings rid of their accepted commentaries, and eventually to a break between orthodox Catholicism and the Reformation, headed in France by Calvin. The Reformation generated new civil wars, which culminated in horrors of all kinds. On August 23, 1572, thousands of French Protestants were massacred in a blood bath known in infamy as Saint-Bartholomew's Night. Assassinations were frequent and claimed the lives of many a leader, including two Kings, Henry III and Henry IV. The latter had been a Huguenot and had won his crown on the battlefield, for the civil war was political as well as religious in character. He converted to Catholicism and was an imaginative and humane ruler whose Edict of Nantes guaranteed the French people a degree of religious tolerance, but his great qualities did not protect him against a fanatic dagger.

The seventeenth century was the century of the great

Louis', Louis XIII and Louis XIV. Louis XIII, aided by Cardinal de Richelieu—another great Frenchman and a model for all statesmen—waged war against all enemies of the state and all the possible roots of rebellion. He and his minister destroyed what was left of the feudal lords' ambition and privileges. They made France a united country in which the power of the central government was obeyed by all and paved the way to the *absolute monarchy* of *Le Roi Soleil,* the Sun King.

Louis XIV (1643–1715) is the most prestigious of all French sovereigns. His countrymen remember that he built the Palace of Versailles and brought great artists and writers to the Court. Mostly for this reason, he gave his name to the century: *Le Siècle de Louis XIV.* Unfortu-

Versailles. *French Embassy*

nately, he waged too many wars, the last of which was too long and too costly. He left France intact, but physically and financially exhausted.

Louis XV (1710–74), known during the early part of his reign as "le Bien-Aimé" or the well-beloved, and Louis XVI (1774–93) were the last of the monarchs of the Old Regime. The former was handsome and intelligent, but left the government to his mistresses, women like Mme. de Pompadour and Mme. Du Barry, and to his ministers, some of whom were extremely weak and unpopular. Meanwhile, the ideas contained in the writings of what has been called the *Age of Enlightenment* were undermining the absolute monarchy and making the minds of the people receptive to change. This change was to come about with singular violence under the hapless, unfortunate Louis XVI.

The French Revolution was brought about by many causes. The immediate one was financial: the French treasury had been drained by the participation of France in wars such as the Seven Years' War and especially the war for American independence. France, on the other hand, was a wealthy country, but the method of collecting taxes was ponderous and often brutal, and the burden fell mostly on the peasants who were least able to pay. The financial situation produced a political crisis about which King Louis XVI and his ministers could do nothing. The Assembly of Notables called in 1787 was equally incapable of action and, in 1789, the King was therefore obliged to convoke the first Parliament ever seen in Europe since the Middle Ages.

Political and social causes converged, since the *bour-*

Battle of the Bastille, the beginning of the French Revolution.
Giraudon

geoisie, or the middle class, which had begun to be enriched by the Industrial Revolution and colonial trade,
and which was not represented in the councils of the
King, wanted power and found in the convocation of a
National Assembly the opportunity to affirm its demands.
The Revolution was also facilitated by a moral crisis and
by an increasingly vocal intelligentsia bent on appraising
and criticizing all traditional institutions.

After ten years of turmoil and wars, a successful general seized the reins of the French Republic. A product of
the French Revolution, Napoleon Bonaparte incarnated

in many ways the conquest of the French Revolution. That is why he is still admired by French liberals as well as conservatives today. After having re-established the territorial integrity of France, which had been invaded by all its neighbors during the Revolutionary troubles, he completely reorganized the civilian and military government of the country. He transformed French society, bringing to power that new aristocracy composed of recently enriched members of the middle class, which had been demanding recognition on the eve of the Revolution.

His main accomplishment, perhaps, was the writing and promulgation of the Civil Code, which was a compromise between the old law and the new one. He also created the Legion of Honor—an honorary order of knighthood to reward service to the state in all fields—the Prefects and the French University, an organization of centralized education which lasted almost unchanged until 1968.

Napoleon certainly wanted to create a European state and, in many ways, was a *European*. He imposed upon all of western Europe the Civil Code which incorporated some of the gains of the Revolution, such as the abolition of class privileges. Most of this reform continued after his fall. The Congress of Vienna, 1815, re-established the old political order and the old King, but left intact the social transformations brought about by the Emperor.

On the morrow of Napoleon's defeat at Waterloo by a coalition of the major European powers, France went back to traditional monarchy. The Bourbon (1814–30) and the Orléans (1830–48) periods marked the reign of the bourgeoisie. These two regimes were destroyed by

short revolutions which were, as a matter of fact, mere
Parisian uprisings and did not greatly change the texture
of French life. The Revolution of 1830 broke out because
Charles X was an obstinate and unintelligent sovereign,
who issued, at the wrong moment, ordinances dissolving
a newly elected Chamber of Deputies possessed of liberal
aspirations. The Revolution of 1848 was likewise caused
by obstinacy and incomprehension, this time on the part
of King Louis-Philippe who, at the end of his reign, did
not understand the wishes of his people and the necessity
for reforms. Once more the Parisians took to the barri-
cades and dethroned the monarch. This time a republican
government was established, but it was short-lived, since
the nephew of Napoleon took over the government. He
did so legally as President, his election having been
favored by the bugbears created by Leftism and Social-
ism and the workers' riots which broke out in Paris in
June 1848.

Louis Napoleon Bonaparte was proclaimed Emperor
after the *coup d'état* of December 2, 1851. The Second
Empire, which was, in general, a period of prosperity,
was to be destroyed by the defeat of the Franco-Prussian
War (1870–71).

The Third Republic (1871–1940) was, on the whole, a
period of slow but definite economic progress. On the eve
of the First World War, France was a rather prosperous
country, with a stable currency. It lent money to the
whole world, especially the Russians who received half of
the total amount involved and never reimbursed their
creditors. France's vast colonial empire included territories in Africa, Asia, Oceania, and the Western Hemi-

sphere. Its republican institutions were solid, even though political life was sometimes troubled as by the Dreyfus case. This famous cause split the country wide open, opposing the superpatriotic believers in authority against the more liberal elements of the electorate. A Jewish army officer, Captain Dreyfus, accused of selling French military secrets to a foreign power, had been sent to the penal colony at Devil's Island. When it became apparent that his condemnation had been a matter of political expediency for men more interested in finding a scapegoat and saving the "honor" of the military than in ascertaining the guilt or innocence of the accused, the great majority of French intellectuals raised their voices against this injustice. Émile Zola, the famous novelist known for realistic novels like *Nana* and *Germinal,* wrote *J'accuse* (I accuse), a violent open letter to the government, and had to go to England in order to escape serving sentence in jail. Dreyfus' case was reopened, however; the captain was cleared of the espionage charges and reinstated, but the whole affair left deep scars and made the French aware of the dangers of anti-Semitism.

France also suffered at that time from excessive economic conservatism and a very low birth rate. Moreover, the international situation was deteriorating, since neighboring Germany had considerably increased its population and its industrial power, and had made its *welt politik* obvious by aggressive interventions in Morocco, the Middle East, and the Balkans. Because of the interplay of alliances, France was more or less obliged to support Serbia and Russia, when Grand Duke Franz Ferdinand of Austria was murdered at Sarajevo. The assassination, of course, was the spark which set fire to an already explosive situation.

France and its Allies finally defeated Germany, but the seeds of World War II were sown at Versailles, in the treaty which put an end to the hostilities. The nations, which had been united in the fight against Germany, found themselves deeply divided when it came to constructing the peace, and each one pursued its particular aims without regard for the common good. All were impoverished and in debt. Furthermore, almost all were left chafing under real or imaginary injustices. Later the Great Depression of 1929 caused considerable suffering in France as well as in other European countries and necessitated the intervention of governments in the field of economy, thus weakening the traditional liberal capitalistic and democratic systems.

The success of extremist parties, Communist and Fascist, outside of France had consequences in France itself: both the strong Communist party and rightist political leagues increased their influence. On the eve of a new war, France was considerably weakened by these internal ideological divisions.

France came into the war, as she had in 1914, because of the binding alliances that she and Britain had made to guarantee their frontiers. After having let Germany rearm and swallow up Austria and Czechoslovakia, France finally had to take a stand, and began the fight against Hitler.

The Second World War was a long, difficult period of trial for the country: defeated, occupied by the enemy, torn by inner conflicts, she finally emerged victorious, but even more ravaged and demoralized than in 1918.

Once more, divisive results of French superindividualism took their toll. A multitude of political parties prevented the Fourth Republic (1944–58) from coping with the problems of organizing efficient political structures. In addition, the colonial era was coming to a close. France, no longer welcome in Indochina, pulled out after a bitter war. In North Africa, the process of decolonization was even more painful since a native population of Europeans, backed by traditionalist army patriots, resisted all efforts to evict them from what they considered their country.

General de Gaulle—the founder of *Free France* and of the French resistance to Hitler and a statesman who was considered by many as the savior of France's honor during World War II—was called to power in the middle of the Algerian War. He put an end to the conflict, settled the North African question, and created the Fifth Republic. A new constitution giving stronger power to the executive was adopted, and stability came back to political life. De Gaulle was re-elected President in 1965. He resigned voluntarily in 1969, after his plan to reform the Senate and grant greater autonomy to the various regions of France was defeated in the national referendum he had requested. He died, one year later (November 9, 1970), and although, at his insistence, his funeral was private and simple, world leaders rendered him formal tribute at a memorial service at Paris' Notre-Dame Cathedral. His successor, Georges Pompidou, on the whole, has followed the general lines of De Gaulle's policies for economic growth and a European balance of power.

Charles de Gaulle. *French Embassy*

III
The French Economy:
From Peasantry
to Industrialization

Napoleon once called England *a nation of shopkeepers.* "The French are peasants," retorted the English. They were right. The fertile soil of France had long made it one of the chief agricultural countries of Europe and had led to the development of an efficient agrarian and social framework. With the coming of the twentieth century, what had been the country's principal strength became a disadvantage as modern industrial demands replaced the old order.

Today, more than two-thirds of the country is still farmland and three and a half million Frenchmen are still peasants—that is, tillers of the soil, quite different from their American counterparts whom they consider contractors rather than farmers. A great number of these peasants work with their families on farms which belonged to their great-grandfathers and make up one of the most hidebound and conservative sections of French economic life, many of them remaining true to the tradition of rugged individualism they inherited from their self-sufficient forebears. On the other hand, there are also large, well-equipped farms, mostly in the North of France, whose owners are quite modern and progressive in their methods.

Farmer selling his produce in the town of Nevers. *Standard Oil, New Jersey*

Another factor which strikes the casual observer is the extraordinary variety of the land. Seen from a plane, much of it looks like a crazy quilt. An official census once counted more than 520 different types of agricultural regions.

The same diversity is found among certain products of the land. There are, for instance, in addition to the

well-known Camembert, Brie, Pont-l'Évêque, Gruyère,
Port-Salut, and *bleu*, 300 classified cheeses. Many of these
are the result of elaborate processing according to cen-
tury-old techniques which make use of the physical conditions of particular regions. A prime example is the
famed Roquefort cheese which is carefully handled and
stored in limestone caves of Roquefort in central France,
which have just the humidity and temperature necessary

A farm in Normandy. *Standard Oil, New Jersey*

to favor the growth of the characteristic penicillium mold. The wide spectrum of wines ranges from the *vins ordinaires* of the Languedoc region to the famous *vins de crus*, or wines so fine that they are identified not only by the general name of the region, such as Bordeaux or Burgundy, where the grapes were grown, but by the precise vineyards where those grapes were picked and the exact year when they were bottled. Weather conditions and the specific quality of the soil are so important that the grapes grown on hills five miles apart can yield wines of very different quality, and the same vineyards can produce excellent wines one year and mediocre ones the next. The Champagne country in the North yields white grapes which are processed according to a formula discovered some two hundred years ago and carefully implemented by highly skilled experts who treat each bottle individually. There is no mass production in the wine industry. There, as well as in the preparation of other spirits and brandies, like cognac and armagnac, infinite care and centuries of tradition ensure the excellence and the reputation of these products all over the world. France's justifiable pride in its superb wines and spirits is nothing new as is evidenced by the *tympan* (recessed panel) of the north portal of the Rheims cathedral, which was built in the twelfth century. Looking at it, the tourist can see a sculpture representing St. Remi, apostle to the Franks, blessing a barrel of wine from the Champagne country.

Many Frenchmen feel that mass production leading to monocultural zones, as in the United States, would debase the quality of the product. It can be feared, of course,

Vineyard in Bordeaux. *French Embassy*

that a reconversion of the French economy, while it would simplify the agricultural map and eliminate unproductive farms, might at the same time destroy some delicious typically French products of quality such as Cavaillon melons, *fraises des bois* (wild, tiny strawberries), exceptional raspberries, truffles, etc.

There are other agricultural problems. Like the United

Vineyard in Bordeaux. *French Embassy*

States, France has a farm surplus. Governments have to
cope with the question of subsidies and with a farm bloc,
which frequently opposes reforms. During a period of almost a century, the wheat lobby was strong enough to
impose upon France a protectionist policy and to mold
the eating habits of the French, who still eat more white
bread than any other people in the world. The wine-

growers are also very hard to discipline and cause the government as many headaches as the wheat farmers. One of the difficulties is how to conciliate protection of the French wines with importation of wines from Algeria, a country which once was part of France and with which there are still very strong economic ties. The fact remains that all the successive administrations have tried to court the farmers, who represent a large number of votes and constitute an element of stability in the country.

Vineyard in Bordeaux. *French Embassy*

A general trend in agriculture, however, is visible: it calls for the increased mechanization of the means of production (the number of tractors has already passed from 30,000 in 1938 to 500,000 in 1971), a greater use of chemicals and insecticides, a better utilization of credit made available through a farmers' bank subsidized by the national government, the gradual elimination of the numerous undersized and inefficient units of production and their replacement by larger, really viable farms.

This will mean duress for many peasants and an increased exodus from the country to the cities. But France will eventually undergo the same fate as other countries in the process of modern industrialization.

The development of French industry has been favored by the presence of rich iron mines in Lorraine (for a long time, France was the largest producer of iron in Europe), bauxite in Provence, and natural gas in the Southwest. Coal exists, in large, but insufficient quantities in the North and on the fringes of the Massif Central. There is, however, a shortage of coking coal and petroleum. Oil has to be imported from the Middle East and the Sahara, and the French also depend on foreign countries for certain metals and raw materials.

French industry has had the help of very good craftsmen, inventors, and men of genius like Louis Pasteur, whose work on the origin of diseases is at the source of all modern immunology; Henri Sainte-Claire Deville, the inventor of a new technique for producing aluminum; Pierre and Marie Curie who discovered radium, and others. It also has a long tradition of quality: silks from Lyons, as well as perfumes from Grasse and glassware from St.

A coal mine near Calais. *French Embassy*

Gobain, have been famous for centuries. In the twentieth century, French industrialists have successfully competed in many areas of the world market. The French cars—Peugeot, Citroën, Renault—have carved out their share of the international trade. Approximately one car out of every two built in France is exported.

The French airplane factories have produced the widely used medium-range *Caravelle* and, together with the

English, are building the *Concorde*. They have also developed some particularly effective military jets, the Dassault *Mirage* and *Mystère*. The network of Air France is one of the widest in the world.

TV may have come to France later than to the United States, but has exceptionally fine picture definition and, once established, made great strides. Today, the French hold patent on a process of color TV, which has the double advantage of high color fidelity, simplicity of concept and operation. It has consequently been adopted by many countries.

There still remain, however, many shadows on the picture of French industry. Too many small family penny-

Supersonic *Concorde* jet airliner. *French Embassy*

pinching enterprises have been hostile to innovation and uninterested in growth and research. Weakness in economic organization, serious class tensions, an inadequate system of collective bargaining, bad politics, excessive social charges, and, until the forties, a low birth rate, have all been factors which hindered the development of industry.

Certain features and even qualities of the French character could also be considered responsible for creating handicaps in that field. Pride in handicraft and meticulous attention to details, for instance, have been distorted or misapplied, with the result that too many producers, proclaiming loudly that they put quality above quantity, have produced too little and failed to use reinvestment as a means of promoting expansion and growth.

The trend in industry, however, just as in agriculture, is toward concentration. The French are trying, through mergers, to create large units, and some of these are quite impressive: Rhône Poulenc (pharmaceutical products and chemicals), St. Gobain (glassware), Pechiney (aluminum), and others are big and still growing.

Moreover, in order to supply the larger needs of an expanding economy and rising living standards, France has been making a massive effort during the last ten years to increase its sources of power through the construction of new dams and hydraulic, thermal, and nuclear plants.

In the field of shipping and maritime trade, the French see clearly the challenge of the immediate future and have already solved its problems. They have expanded shipyards and installed the necessary new equipment to

Hydroelectric stations in eastern France. *United Nations*

build 250,000- to 500,000-ton ultra-automated tankers.
They are well along in the construction of the deep-chan-
nel, life-berth new port facilities to handle the mammoth
boats and the new-fashioned *container*-type of shipping.
Ports like St. Nazaire, Nantes, Dunkirk, and Le Havre on
the Channel, La Ciotat, La Seyne, and above all Mar-

seilles-Fos on the Mediterranean, have been considerably enlarged. Marseilles-Fos, which is the main point of entry for France's imports of crude oil and the Mediterranean terminal for the European pipeline now working at full capacity, is the only European port able to accommodate tankers of more than 200,000 tons and has equipment able to unload 7,000 tons of crude oil an hour.

Unloading docks for crude oil from Kuwait. *French Embassy*

The French markets are also moving with the times. In Paris, for instance, the Halles, that sprawling, noisy, odorous, traffic-congesting, picturesque food market, which Émile Zola, in a famous novel, called "the belly of Paris," was replaced in 1969 by Europe's largest and most modern food market, a $110 million, 1,480-acre spread at Rungis, five miles outside Paris, close to Orly airport.

The growth of the French economy has been helped, in recent years, by the development of credit. One out of every three washing machines and one out of every two TV sets and cars are bought on credit. Credit cards (*Carte Bleue, Diners' Club*) were introduced during the late sixties, and many Frenchmen are doing what Americans have been doing for decades, buying now, paying later. France is still far below the United States in that connection, but today it uses credit more than any other European country, except Britain.

The decline of agriculture and the growth of industry and trade have favored the development of the cities.

Greater Paris, which had 900,000 inhabitants in 1830, had grown to 9,000,000 in 1971. Over the same period of time, the population of Marseilles increased 800 per cent. A number of communities which, at the turn of the century, were merely large towns, such as Caen, Orléans, Rheims, are today cities of 100,000 or more. There are now forty-nine French cities with more than 100,000 residents. By 1985, there will be at least sixty in that population range.

France has entered the era of urban revolution. As the famous architect Le Corbusier wrote some years ago, "for

Aerial view of Paris. *French Embassy*

thousands of years, French cities had found their equilibrium on the basis of how far, in an hour, a man, a horse or a bull could walk. Now they have to adapt themselves to the rhythm of fast-moving cars, aircraft, and the immeasurable speed of the telegraph, telephone, and radio." The French have been facing these challenges by planning and developing new communities in unpopulated and economically viable parts of the country. In the spring of 1969, the newspaper *France Soir* began a report with these words:

"A peaceful little country churchyard surrounded by an old stone wall; very near to it, a small wood with singing blackbirds, open field all around. And then, one day, there was an immense work site, with cranes and bulldozers and cement-mixers. It was the beginning of a new city—Evry—in the Department of Essonne." A few months later, Evry, a city built on the slopes of the valley of the Seine, numbered about 10,000 inhabitants.

Satellite cities are also being planned around Lyons, Lille, and other economic centers.

Some problems subsist which handicap French economy as a whole. The first of these is the still inadequate means of communications: France has a fairly good system of railroads—subsidized by the state and operating in the red—and a few clover-leaf intersections and highway interchanges, but turnpikes have been built at a snail's pace. Secondly, there is an imbalance between exports and imports: France imports too much, exports too little. Tourism and other "hidden exports" are not sufficient to produce an equilibrium. Thirdly, some regions are trailing in their expansion: Brittany, for instance, exports only 290 francs' worth of goods per year per inhabitant, which is five times less than the national average.

The government is conscious of these problems and is trying to solve them. But solutions can probably be found only within a European union, and it is an evident fact that other countries (for example, Germany and England) which are partners or future partners of France in the Common Market—a good start toward European unity —are anxious to preserve their national interests and often unwilling to follow the leadership of France or to accept her views.

IV
The French Version
of Democracy

It is probably easier to find out what kind of democracy France is *not* than to define its special brand of regime. It is not a "popular democracy" with a one-party rule. It is not a "representative democracy" with an elected President who leads the country as the American President does. It is neither a "parliamentary democracy" like England, with a two-party system, where the Prime Minister is, at the same time, the head of the majority and the chief executive; nor is it a democracy of the Scandinavian type, with a strongly socialized state supervising a "consumer society." It is not a "town-meeting democracy," not a "fragmentary cantonal democracy," like Switzerland. It is not a regime based on a strict separation of powers, even though the theory of *séparation des pouvoirs* (separation of powers) originated with Montesquieu's writings in eighteenth-century France. Moreover, whereas the executive and legislative powers are elective, the judiciary is not. District attorneys, magistrates, and judges are civil servants, named from lists of qualified candidates, and must have a legal formation attested by examinations and diplomas. Frenchmen would not trust any system appointed on election, which might subject the judiciary to the vicissitudes of politics.

Changing of the guard at the Élysée Palace, home of France's President. *French Embassy*

French democracy is, at best, a kind of compromise between other types, and presently its features are rather vaguely drawn, because the constitution of 1958 is still in the process of being tested and, possibly, amended.

In order to understand the French system of government, one must remember some historical and psychological factors. The French like change and have had many revolutions, but they also respect tradition. They are fond of justice, equality, and freedom, but they also long for order and stability. They like "nuances" (subtleties) and could not live under a one or two-party system. Under the Third and Fourth republics, there were as many as thirty different parties or schools of political thought. More recently, there has been a reduction in the number of parties and a simplification of the political map, but there were still seven qualified candidates in the last presidential election, and there are at least ten major parties which elect mayors and members of city and department councils and send deputies and senators to Parliament.

Traditionally the Rightists oppose the Leftists. The former are not always conservatives, but they are attached to traditional values. They are, perhaps, more realistic than the opposition. The latter are more sentimental and, generally speaking, more *liberal*. In between is the Center, which leans at times toward the Right and at times toward the Left and is at all times essential to obtaining an electoral majority. Most of the governments of the last fifty years were formed by coalitions, either of the Moderate Left and the Center or of the Right and Center parties.

Workmen erect election posters. *French Embassy*

Party labels, however, should not be taken too literally. Some so-called Rightists have been, just like the English Tories, much more liberal than their Leftist adversaries. A Leftist party, for instance, called the *Radical Socialists,* has never been socialistic and hardly ever radical. Labels are for electoral use: no one can be elected who does not proclaim himself a good Republican, a sincere Democrat and, if possible, a man with Socialist leanings and who does not come out strongly against something, preferably against the *status quo* or the *ins*. It has even been said that those Frenchmen who vote for the Leftists, and especially for the Communist party, are often merely protesting against the *status quo*, rather than expressing a vote of confidence in Marxist or Leninist ideas.

The present constitution was adopted by a popular referendum in which 79.5 per cent of the electorate expressed their approval of a strong executive in contrast with the weak unstable government of the Fourth Republic. Virtually all parties are now agreed on maintaining this constitution, including the presidential system, although politicians may differ on how the presidential powers should be exercised.

Under the Third and Fourth republics, the President was elected by Parliament and supposed to be a kind of "umpire" between parliamentary groups, but, beginning with General de Gaulle, French Presidents have been elected by direct, universal suffrage. They are voted in for a seven-year term and have broad executive powers. They nominate Prime Ministers who must be confirmed by Parliament, negotiate and ratify treaties which also must be approved by Parliament, preside over the Council of Ministers, promulgate the laws passed by Parliament, may submit drafted laws to referendum and may assume, in time of crisis, exceptional, but temporary, powers.

The strong hand of General de Gaulle sometimes concealed the fact that there is a French Parliament regularly elected by universal suffrage and composed of a National Assembly and a Senate. Even De Gaulle was unable to cut the powers of the High Chamber, also called a "Chamber of reflexion"; in fact, his resignation was due, at least partly, to his inability to make France a unicameral country.

The Prime Minister must work in close harmony with the President and, especially when his majority is made up of a coalition, with Parliament. This is probably the most original and possibly the weakest feature of the French system. But the French, on the whole, do not dislike it, because they feel that they have there a system of checks and balances which can limit abuses of power on the part of President, Prime Minister, and Parliament. They cannot forget that a President or a Prime Minister may be endowed with too strong a personality and seize the power as did both Napoleon Bonaparte and his nephew, Napoleon the Third. Parliaments, on the other hand, have their *prima donnas* and are often talkative, unruly, and inefficient.

No regime is better than its leaders. Often in the past, except in times of crises when there was a Clemenceau, a Poincaré, or a De Gaulle to lead the country, politicians have not been equal to their task. But France, in fact, did not suffer too much from the inadequacy of its apparent leaders, because the real power belonged to a more efficient body called *l'Administration*—i.e., the civil servants. It has frequently been said that France was badly governed but well administered. This was certainly the case under the Third Republic and possibly the Fourth.

At the level of local government, elected mayors and *conseils municipaux*, or city councils, were, on the whole, quite adequate for their limited responsibilities.

At the national level, public servants were well trained,

honest, and devoted to their jobs. Heads of services in the ministries and *préfets* at the head of *départements* (i.e., local administrative units) were usually extremely responsible and served the state well. Their only serious handicap was the usual one inherent in bureaucracies: the administrative machine was sometimes heavy, difficult to move, unable to react to the challenge of new problems. In order to try and improve this situation, the Fourth Republic created a *School of National Administration*, the E.N.A., which recruited students through stiff competitive examinations, put the emphasis on intelligence, experience and imagination and gave the state some of its best technocrats.

France, however, is still suffering from a high dose of centralization and state monopolies brought about by Napoleon and developed by his successors. Even today, there are 3,500,000 Frenchmen employed and salaried by the state. Not all of them are doing a realistic job: the state tobacco monopoly, for instance, still makes chewing tobacco, even though less and less people chew. The central power is supposed to be the source of all knowledge and decision. For a long time even little problems of a small community had to be referred to Paris for a decision, and the answer, too often, was too long in coming. Monopolies, on the other hand, make for a lack in the spirit of competition, of emulation, of progress.

In the past, strong central ministries had rendered countless services in many fields, but the need for decentralization was never felt more strongly than during the sixties when the state instituted a number of reforms, the results of which are yet to be ascertained. This has been particularly true in the field of national education. The French university, which was overcentralized, over-bureaucratized, is now being divided into smaller, auton-omous units. Funds are now made available to those small units and can be spent without asking Paris for authoriza-tion.

More power also is being given to regional organiza-tions. Generally speaking, the change is toward a liberali-zation and decentralization of the whole system, but also toward the regrouping of a plethora of units of inadequate size. Whereas Great Britain has only 1,854 townships, there are, in France, 38,000 *communes,* 30,000 of which have less than 2,000 inhabitants. This is largely the result of the erstwhile agricultural character of France, where numerous farms clustered around a village to form a small community. Elected mayors, *conseils municipaux* (city councils), and *conseils généraux* are now trying to co-operate locally for the best interest of a whole region.

The French concept of democracy includes the notion of the social responsibility of the state. A system of *social security* was adopted by France long before the United States considered it. It covers unemployment insurance, family subsidies, consisting of a certain sum for each child and for the mother who chooses to remain at home to bring up her children rather than seek outside employ-ment, and medical aid which pays between 70 per cent and 75 per cent of the patient's expenses. Old-age pen-sions, on the other hand, are at this time quite low, and many people feel that they are far from adequate.

A complete picture of French democracy should also include facts about the press. The unusually large number of independent newspapers is a reflection of the large number of possible political positions. Journalists are politically committed, resolutely outspoken, and convinced of their mission to lead and influence opinion as well as give information. Not only *L'Humanité*, mouthpiece for the Communist party, but also such conservative papers as *Le Figaro* and *Le Monde* interpret the news and are politically *engagés* (engaged). The cartoons and satirical articles of *Le Canard Enchaîné* systematically deride governmental foibles and have violently attacked unpopular officialdom even during the mandate of President de Gaulle who is supposed to have read it faithfully and to have sometimes appreciated the quality of the irony and satire directed against his ministers.

Worth mentioning also is the involvement of an increasing proportion of young people in the political life of the country. They are questioning the part they are being trained to play in a society of which they do not always totally approve. It is interesting to note, in this connection, that civic education and the study and discussion of political structures have recently been added to secondary school curricula.

V
Social Classes
and Class Differences

There was a time, under the Old Regime, when French society was clearly divided into privileged classes, the aristocracy and clergy, and a non-privileged class, the Third Estate, which included all those who worked on the land as well as tradesmen, craftsmen, people involved in industry and commerce and most members of the liberal professions. The French Revolution of 1789 has not entirely done away with class differences: there are still noblemen inordinately proud of their rank, even though the word *de* preceding a name is not necessarily a mark of nobility. There are aristocrats who sneer at the bourgeois, members of the "haute bourgeoisie" (upper middle class) who sneer at little shopkeepers, and white-collar workers who look down on blue-collar laborers. It has been said that class differences have never been sincerely abandoned in France since the general assumption —and especially the prevalent opinion among the all-powerful Parisian *concierges* (doorkeepers)—is that such stratification is necessary and practical.

There are still a few thousand French aristocrats who trace their titles to a more or less distant past and who consider each other proportionately more or less distinguished. Since the Revolution of 1830, however, they have never regained political influence. A handful of these "blue-blooded" persons, as described in the novels of Balzac, Stendhal, and Proust, live on the Left Bank of Paris, along the Faubourg St.-Germain. Many more dwell in the country where they form a generally impoverished gentry.

Members of the nobility are mainly to be found in two careers: the army and the diplomatic corps. Some generals of the two World Wars—De Curières de Castelnau, De Lattre de Tassigny, Leclerc de Hauteclocque, to name a few—were true aristocrats; but they were a small minority scattered among the more plebeian members of the military caste, and the same was true in diplomatic circles too.

The bourgeois notables took hold of economic power after the Revolution of 1789, and kept it through various political regimes, showing a great capacity for adjustment to divers types of constitutional monarchies or republics.

Below the high bourgeoisie, the middle and small bourgeoisie include a great number of Frenchmen: teachers, minor officials, bureaucrats, tradesmen. This last category is well represented, since there are still some 400,000 stores with annual earnings of less than $4,000 each.

Today, the high and middle bourgeoisie form a cohesive group imbued with a certain set of values: they believe in hard work; in the importance of private property; in liberalism in the old sense of the word, i.e., *laissez faire* (noninterference), freedom from the control of the state; in frugality, common sense, and careful family and budget planning.

These values and virtues can often degenerate so that

the French bourgeois is often represented in literature and in the theater as narrow-minded, egotistical, avaricious, and smug. But, at their best, the members of this large middle class make up the backbone of France.

There are in France approximately six million industrial workers. Working conditions and paid vacations are determined by law. The forty-four-hour week was also made mandatory by the state in 1969.

Unskilled laborers, who are considered members of a kind of subproletariat, still have low salaries. At the end of 1971, the minimum salary, known as the S.M.I.G., a figure constantly scrutinized and reviewed by the government, was the equivalent of no more than eighty cents an hour. A 22-year-old unskilled laborer in the provinces may make one hundred and twenty-five dollars a month. Fifteen years later, he may not be earning much more than one hundred and fifty dollars.

In 1971, the average salary for French workers as a whole was approximately the equivalent of one dollar an hour. Skilled laborers, who work in large factories, earn more. The salary of a machinist, for instance, may be between two hundred and twenty-five and two hundred and seventy-five dollars a month, which is about the European average for the same kind of work.

It must be remembered, however, that these figures represent only a portion of the workman's real earnings since he receives social benefits, including family subsidies, and reduced fares on public transportation and trains as well as special rates in company stores and restaurants. Education is free at all levels, even the most advanced, and deserving university students can expect to receive financial support for living expenses and books during their years of study.

A great many, but not all, salaried members of the working class belong to trade unions. The most important of these are the *Confédération Générale du Travail* (General Federation of Labor), or C.G.T., which calls itself *apolitical* but is strongly communist-oriented, and two other decidedly Leftist groups, *Force Ouvrière* (Labor Power), or F.O. and the *Confédération Française Démocrate du Travail* (French Democratic Federation of Labor), referred to as the C.F.D.T. These unions are entirely different from their American counterparts in that they are much more actively interested in ideologies and engaged in political maneuvering. The struggle for material benefits is real, but is subordinated to an indoctrination which aims at making the workers aware of the unequal distribution of wealth and the discrepancy between affluence and poverty. On the other hand, the events of May 1968, during which activist leaders tried to "politize" them, showed plainly that individual union members, far from being revolutionary, are not in the least interested in abstract ideological principles, but seek primarily to attain a higher standard of living and enjoy the benefits of that same *consumer society* so despised by anarchist *gauchists* (leftists).

The lowest stratum of French society is probably the peasant body, comprising small landowners and agricultural workers. They earn very little and are generally hostile to the necessary evolution of the economy. They have been called and are, in a way, a *condemned class*.

Labor union meeting. *French Embassy*

Twenty per cent of the agricultural-class peasants vote communistic because they are a rural proletariat and the Communists channel their discontent. They are, however, anything but internationally minded Marxists, and most of them retain a deep love and attachment for the land.

VI
France,
Mother of the Arts

"France, Mother of the Arts," said the sixteenth-century poet Joachim Du Bellay. As a matter of fact, from prehistoric times until the present day, France seems to have been one of the favored nations for the arts in their many diverse forms.

Art made its appearance on French soil, at the time of the cave men, with the magnificent paintings of Lascaux and other Périgord prehistoric dwellings. Thousands of years later, the Romans left their mark with such monuments as the arenas of Arles and of Lutèce, as Paris was once called, triumphal arches like that of Orange, the *Maison Carrée* (Square House) in Nîmes and many others. During the tenth, eleventh, and twelfth centuries, the Romanesque gave such beautiful abbeys as the *Mont St.-Michel,* the one in Caen known as the *Abbaye-aux-Hommes* and churches such as *Notre-Dame la Grande* in Poitiers and *St. Foy* in Conques. Then came the Gothic churches, like those of Laon, Paris, Chartres, Amiens, Rheims, etc., with their ribbed vaults, pointed arches, flying buttresses and stained glass windows.

At the same time, French artists illuminated manuscripts and Books of Hours with highly colored miniatures, representing religious and secular subjects, and

Cathedral at Amiens. *French Embassy*

thus brought into being what became known as the
French art. Dante, in his *Purgatorio,* refers to this when
he says: *Quell' arte ch' alluminar chiamata e in Parisi!*
(That art which in Paris is called illumination!)

During the Renaissance, the Kings built the chateaus of
the Loire valley such as Blois, Azay-le-Rideau, Loches,
Chambord, etc. In the seventeenth century, Mansart and
Le Nôtre created for Louis XIV the majestic ensemble of
Versailles. The eighteenth century saw the triumph of a
lighter, more intimate style. The last two centuries were
marked by the appearance of many movements, Roman-
ticism, Realism, Neo-Gothic, Impressionism, etc., which
all had great French representatives. We have only to

think of Cézanne, who is generally considered the father of modern art.

Today it is almost impossible to visit any part of the country without encountering one or many examples of this rich artistic heritage. In Paris, for instance, the tourist can find art of the early Gauls at the Musée de Cluny, beautiful Gothic churches, such as Notre-Dame de Paris,

Notre-Dame Cathedral. *Air France*

Eiffel Tower. *Air France*

O.R.T.F. Radio and Television Building. *French Embassy*

celebrated in Victor Hugo's famous internationally known historical novel, *The Hunchback of Notre-Dame,* as well as daring nineteenth- and twentieth-century constructions like the Eiffel Tower, or the interesting examples of modern architecture which shelter the O.R.T.F., as the French Radio and Television Organization is usually called, the U.N.E.S.C.O., and, at the *Rond Point de la Défense,* a traffic circle northwest of Paris, the Nobel Tower, and the Exhibition Hall known under the initials C.N.I.T., which stand for *Centre National des Industries Techniques* (National Center of Technical Industries).

In the provinces, there are hundreds of *villes d'art* (museum cities), old churches, small châteaus, and other historical sites. The French Government, supported by the French public and sometimes by American benefactors, as was the case for Versailles, subsidizes, restores, and tries to protect by law this patrimony. Recently the Ministry of Culture, under the direction of writer André Malraux, had old Paris houses and monuments cleansed of the accumulated grime of centuries, giving a new life and new beauty to a now resplendent city, especially to the Conciergerie, Notre-Dame, the Louvre, and other landmarks of the capital which suddenly appeared marvelously bright and revealed unsuspected details of sculpture and texture.

When considering the many forms of art which have come to vigorous new life in France during the past fifty years, one should not forget the making of tapestries, an ancient craft which was launched anew by a great French poet and painter, Jean Lurçat. The porcelain industry also had long flourished in France, with Sèvres and Li-

Inside the Louvre. *French Embassy*

moges as its focal points. Today, it continues strong and vital, and Limoges has acquired fame in a second area, that of enamels. Craftmanship, allied with taste and a flair for the modern, characterizes numerous industries and attracts leading artists to centers like Vallauris, near

Cannes, where fine pottery bears prestigious signatures, not the least of which is Picasso.

Art finds its way into the daily life of everyone who uses the post office and mails, since in the past few years, there have been spectacularly beautiful postage stamps reproducing with singular felicity some of the masterpieces found in French museums—works ranging from the prehistoric paintings of the Lascaux caves to the medieval miniatures of the Book of Hours of the Duc of Berry and the great paintings of Delacroix, Ingres, Toulouse-Lautrec, Renoir, Chagall, Matisse, Braque, Dufy, and others.

It has long been a tradition for artists from everywhere to go to Paris to try and absorb its atmosphere. They have usually found in the French capital two things which were often lacking in their own countries: intellectual freedom and artistic companionship. True international flavor can be perceived in such places as Montparnasse, and it has rightly been said that the *école de Paris* (Paris school), in the first part of the twentieth century was, in fact, an international school, famous not only for French artists but for foreign-born painters like Utrillo, Picasso, Miro, Van Dongen, Dali, and hundreds of others.

French literature has a vigorous tradition which goes almost as far back as the language itself and by the twelfth century, had produced a recognized and resounding masterpiece, the epic *Chanson de Roland* (*Song of Roland*). The troubadours of France introduced lyric poetry and the code of courtly love which strongly influenced the literature of the North with its stories of knighthood and adventure. Beginning with the Renaissance, there was always at least one great French writer whose fame extended beyond the frontier of country and time: Rabelais, Montaigne, Descartes, Voltaire, Rousseau, Hugo, Balzac, Baudelaire, Flaubert, Zola, Anatole France, Camus, to name only a few. World War II saw the development of the movement known as *existentialism* which, under the influence of Jean-Paul Sartre's brilliant essays, plays, and novels, exerted its influence well beyond the boundaries of France and French thought.

In the twentieth century, France, with twelve laureates, has received the Nobel Prize for Literature more often than any other country. Writers so honored include novelists Anatole France, Romain Rolland, and André Gide, poet Saint-John Perse, essayists and dramatists Albert Camus and Jean-Paul Sartre, philosopher Henri Bergson. The 1969 Nobel Prize for Literature was awarded to the author of the internationally known play, *Waiting for Godot*, Irish-born Samuel Beckett, who has lived in France for most of his life and writes in French.

There is in France a striking interest in literature and writers, as witnessed by the great number of libraries and bookshops, which were among the first stores to open their doors again after the air raids of World War II and by the large quantity of newspapers, journals, and magazines reflecting every type of opinion and preoccupation. The daily press gives detailed accounts of numerous literary prizes and stories about writers and books. No newspaper or journal is without a book section and a literary critic. We might add that among the better and most popular programs on radio and television are those which deal with authors and their problems.

Living writers are passionately discussed, and it is easy to see that official recognition has been given to those of the past by looking at the names of the streets in any French city, big or small: rue Racine, rue Michelet, rue Paul Valéry, avenue Victor Hugo, etc. . . .

True, the best sellers, in France like everywhere else, are not always the best works published, but the fact remains that classics and other good books are bought, borrowed, and read by millions every year.

Outside of France, the best recent French writers are immediately translated and often are the subject of doctoral dissertations or theses, even before they have been recognized by the general public at home. French contemporary literature is taught in many foreign universities and almost every contemporary writer of mark has been invited to lecture abroad, from Jules Romains and André Maurois to Camus, Sartre, Natalie Sarraute, and Alain Robbe-Grillet.

France has also made great contributions to the arts of theater, motion pictures, and music. Among the great "classics" which are played in repertory theaters all over the world, the most famous names are perhaps, in the seventeenth century, those of Molière, Corneille, and Racine; in the eighteenth, those of Marivaux and Beaumarchais; in the nineteenth, those of Victor Hugo and Edmond Rostand. Works of French contemporary dramatists such as Camus, Sartre, Beckett, Anouilh, and Ionesco are often produced on and off Broadway and in American colleges.

As to the motion picture, which was born in France with
Louis Lumière, it developed into what is frequently called
the "seventh art" with the help of such directors as Jacques
Feyder; Jean Renoir, who made *Grande Illusion;* Jean
Cocteau, creator of *Orpheus;* Tati who gave us *Mr. Hulot's
Holiday;* Godard; Truffaut; and Lelouch, responsible for
A Man and a Woman.

The origin of French music coincides with the advent
of Western music during the Middle Ages, when an impressive array of composers, Perotinus Magnus, Guillaume
de Machaut, etc., furnished religious and secular com-
positions which can still be heard today. In the thirteenth
century, Adam de la Halle produced what may well be
the first musical comedy, *Le Jeu de Robin et Marion (The
Play of Robin and Marion).* The songs of the troubadours,
the works of well-known or anonymous authors, inaugu-
rated a form of entertainment continued through the
centuries by such composer-singers as Aristide Bruant
and Yvette Guilbert, and today by internationally famous
singers and songwriters like Brassens and Aznavour.

During the seventeenth century, the collaboration of
Molière and Lulli in ballets and comedies did much to
further the development of comic opera and opera.

Today, in spite of the fact that music has for a long time
rarely figured adequately in school curricula and only
recently made its appearance, as an optional subject, in
the baccalaureate examinations, it is encouraged outside
of school through specialized and highly selective con-
servatories throughout the land. The French Government
shows its interest in the musical arts by subsidizing the

Paris Conservatory of Music, two national music theaters, the Opéra and the Opéra Comique, and certain official bands and symphony orchestras, including l'Orchestre de Paris. *Les Jeunesses Musicales de France* (French Musical Youth), a vast organization open to all who love music, sponsors concerts, and makes the important events of the musical year available to its members at reasonable rates.

In recent times Claude Debussy, who popularized the whole-tone scale, and Maurice Ravel were leading writers of impressionist music. Darius Milhaud incorporated South American rhythms in his music, Messiaen, Varese, and Boulez are among the best-known modern composers.

L'Opéra. *Air France*

VII
French Customs:
Some Things Old,
Some Things New,
Some Things Borrowed...

For a long time, France has been considered a static traditionalist country. On the covers of guidebooks for tourists (as well as text books for United States high schools), there appeared old Breton women with quaint high *coiffes* (headdresses) and Arlesian girls dancing in the streets. This picture was not entirely wrong, since France was an old country and most Frenchmen did not reject or belittle the patrimony they had inherited from their ancestors. Things, however, have changed during the last generation, and there is today a coexistence of the old and the new, the new becoming more and more apparent and gradually displacing the old.

Tradition, of course, is still strong. In France family relations, for instance, are still based, to some extent, on definite parental authority. There are still craftsmen who make *martinets* (cat o' nine tails) and parents who buy those whips to punish disobedient children. Public education is still based upon the Napoleonic idea that the state knows best, and that the aim of education is to form the mind, to develop good judgment and a highly critical, rationalist approach to life. Examinations at the high school and college level are given on programs of studies

Breton women with quaint headdresses. *French Embassy*

fixed by the state. Students of a *lycée* (school) or a university are awarded degrees valid and of equal worth throughout the land. There is no such thing yet as the American system of adult education or education for the masses. A majority of Frenchmen is still convinced that, for the nation to prosper, the centralized bureaucratic system of education conceived at the time of Napoleon for a bourgeois *élite* needs only to be adapted to the needs and demands of the modern world.

In many fields, tradition often stands very much in the path of progress. Many industrialists do not like to open their books or to hire public relations services. Many businessmen and farmers do not like to borrow, many bankers do not like to extend credit. It has been said that French investors tend to behave like their ancestors in the first part of the nineteenth century: rather than invest in the stock market, they prefer to buy land, houses, apartments, or gold. These purchases represent more than 58 per cent of the patrimony of the French, as against 39 per cent in 1923; stocks and bonds make up only 17 per cent of French wealth. Reliability and stability are deemed much more important than a high yield. The average Frenchman, moreover, knows little about modern economic theories and is not interested in them.

There are other ways in which tradition prevails. Most working people would be unwilling to give up their one- or two-hour lunch period, even if their working day were to end earlier. They do not care to go on vacation in June or September, because traditionally August is *the* month for a vacation. Hotel owners, who should know better, hesitate before modernizing their facilities. First of all, it would be too costly and, besides, they do not consider it necessary to improve *material* comfort, since the French love to think that they are above caring for such down-to-earth matters and seek only spiritual advantages. . . .

On the other hand, tradition, of course, may ensure quality of the highest order. Such is certainly the case with respect to craftsmanship, which is very frequently quite excellent and much more satisfactory than what one finds abroad.

The art of cooking benefits from a tradition enriched by generations of lovers of food and wine. A meal, in France, is not a snack. It takes time to prepare, time to eat, time to appreciate, time to digest and talk about. The French like to discuss cooking, recipes, and restaurants (rated one, two, or three stars), and they devote a good deal of their time to doing just that. Some statistics indicate that they spend as much as 40 per cent of their income on food and restaurants.

Tradition prevails also in relations between people. Whereas in America one concludes a letter with a short formula such as "Sincerely yours" or "Best regards," in France this would be impossible. There are, instead, an infinite number of different formulas each of which, a paragraph long, is especially conceived for a particular situation and takes into account such considerations as social rank and the private regard the sender has for the receiver. For instance, someone writing a bread-and-butter letter might end it somewhat like this: "I should like to thank you, *chère madame* (dear madam), for your kindness and beg you to find here, with my sincere gratitude, the expression of my most respectful regards."

Traditional leisure-time occupations have not changed much in the twentieth century. In the provinces, they still play *boules* or *pétanque*—a form of pinless bowling—on the public squares, and checkers or *dames* or, in the cafés, an indigenous card game named *belote*.

The most popular spectator sports are also the same as fifty years ago: soccer, rugby, tennis, track, cycling, and horse racing. Every year in July, the famed international bicycle race, the "Tour de France," is followed as avidly

Outdoor bowling. *French Embassy*

Sailboat races. *French Embassy*

Horse racing (Hippodrome at Longchamps). *French Embassy*

in newspapers and on television as the World Series in the United States. Horse racing is not the sport of kings, but one of the most popular sports the common man. Off-track betting is a monopoly of the government which runs the "Tiercé," a bet on the three horses to come in first in a major race, which plays the same role as the football pool in England. Swimming is also popular in France, even though it is not extensively practiced, and Americans are always surprised to see how many French children have never learned to swim.

The Tour de France. *French Embassy*

In spite of the hold of tradition, France has known a great many changes during the past twenty years.

The principal cause for these changes has been the demographic factor. France used to be a country of middle-aged and older people, a land afflicted with a stationary birth rate. After the Second World War, thanks to an enormous increase in natality, France went from forty million inhabitants in 1939 to fifty million in 1968 and emerged as a country of young people—young people who make their voices heard and with whom their elders have learned to count.

Before the two World Wars, the French traveled very little. The advent of the cheap car, especially the 2 CV Citroën and the 4 CV Renault, allowed many Frenchmen to discover their own country and to explore the world. Just before World War II, the law granted all factory workers a four-week annual paid vacation. Today, many Frenchmen enjoy a five-week vacation and they take advantage of it to visit Europe, to become members by the thousands of charter-travel clubs such as the Club Méditerranée, which has installations all over the world. Every summer Frenchmen are to be found in Greece, their vacation dreamland number 1, according to a recent international survey, as well as in Yugoslavia, Italy, Tunisia, Morocco, Crimea, Tahiti, the United States, and Canada, etc., and, because of favorable monetary rates of exchange, they cross the Pyrénées by hundreds of thousands to visit Spain and Portugal.

Class consciousness, which was always extremely strong in France, might well be lessening because of these factors. Another leveling influence is the fact that students and young people of well-to-do families seeking greater financial independence are beginning, like young Americans, to take summer jobs which would have been deemed unthinkable even ten or fifteen years ago.

The French have also enthusiastically gone in for the material improvement of life. Forty per cent of the population own or rent washing machines, refrigerators, and TV sets. Housewives, abandoning local market places and small shops, go to big *supermarchés* (supermarkets). They no longer dislike living in high buildings, and skyscrapers, totally unknown in France until World War II, have transformed the skylines of all major cities, including Paris.

The French are in the process of discovering that the telephone, superhighways, and computers are essential elements of progress. They are even doing something about it.

The field of economy itself is being brought to the attention of the public through the agency of the leading newspapers, which now devote considerable space to what they formally ignored.

The young have superimposed their taste in entertainment on adult leisure-time occupations. They favor jazz and rock-and-roll music. Jukeboxes have been installed in almost every café of big and small cities and villages. Young Frenchmen enjoy sports and are probably more gifted in the field than their elders. They like to drive motorcycles or bicycles equipped with a small motor. In summer, so many of them try their skill at sailing that the enormous increase in marinas has been one of the most extraordinary developments in the past few years. Winter

Superhighway. *French Embassy*

finds them in increasing numbers taking advantage of the skiing facilities of the mountain ranges.

The modernization of France is visible in other unexpected areas. The Catholic Church, which for years had been extremely conservative and associated with middleclass respectability, has become intensely involved in finding acceptable solutions to modern world problems. Some priests and nuns have left their cloisters to work in factories, share the daily life of the people, and give their message directly to those who might not seek them out in the confines of church buildings.

Finally, there is an increased consciousness of the national contemporary problems. Books like *Le Défi américain* (*The American Challenge*), a best seller in France since 1967, stress the defects of the French system and suggest ways of improving the situation. They advise developing teamwork, broadening research, filling the management and marketing gaps, and educating the general public.

The coexistence of the old, the new, and the borrowed can easily be seen in Paris where there is one fortune-teller for two hundred inhabitants, and a Champs Elysées shop where many individual Frenchmen go to have their horoscope cast by an IBM computer.

Old section of Paris. *French Embassy*

VIII
France and the U.S.A.:
A Happy Marriage?

In telling and retelling the story of French-American relations, writers on both sides of the Atlantic have liked to use the image of a "happy marriage" between two countries which never warred against each other and three times fought together against a common enemy. Actually, although there have always been strong sentimental ties between France and the United States, there have also been a good many misunderstandings. The course of that "love story" has not always been smooth.

It all started with the days when French explorers, missionaries, and soldiers opened up and colonized the New World. In 1524, Jean de Verrazano, a Franco-Italian navigator sent by the King of France, discovered the site of New York. He gave it the name of *Angoulesme*, in honor of François I, duke of Angoulême. Then came Jacques Cartier, Marquette, Jolliet, and Cavelier de la Salle who took possession of a large territory later called *Louisiane* as a homage to Louis XIV. Hundreds of old French names remind us, even now, of the presence of the French in that region of America: Coeur d'Alène, Eau Claire, Prairie du Chien, Pierre, Des Moines, Belleville, Cadillac. In the United States, there are at least seven urban communities named Paris!

The North American continent was disputed between the French and the English, and when the American colonists revolted against the Crown, the French were their natural allies. Besides political considerations, there was a strong current of sympathy between the American "elite" and the French intellectuals of the "Age of Enlightenment." Jefferson, for instance, was a great admirer of Voltaire. The French loved Benjamin Franklin, the "Good Quakers," the "Free" World, and Utopian Pennsylvania, where, supposedly, sugar flowed from the trees and eternal peace reigned in a tax-free land.

When the Revolution broke out, many young French volunteers took part in the conflict. The best known was the Marquis de La Fayette who left his young wife and his family, paid for his own equipment, and made such a notable contribution to the cause of American freedom that he and his descendants were given honorary citizenship.

The French King, Louis XVI, also officially helped the colonies at great cost to French taxpayers and, ironically, his participation in the costly and successful American Revolution was to prove, for financial and ideological reasons, the first step toward the French Revolution which cost him his life.

Even before the end of the Revolutionary War, however, France and America came close to breaking off diplomatic relations; the colonists made a separate peace with England and never satisfactorily settled their war debts with France. Shortly afterward the French engaged in a violent Revolution, which the moderates who had founded the new American Republic found too strong to

Marquis
de La Fayette.
French Embassy

swallow. When the Girondins sent "Citizen Genet" to Philadelphia, the French envoy soon became *persona non grata:* Americans did not relish revolutionary propaganda. Washington and his successors decided on a course of isolationism which was to last long after the death of the Great Founder.

French-American relations improved sharply when Bonaparte sold Louisiana to Jefferson. The French were no longer a danger or a menace to the United States. On the contrary, at the time of the Purchase, residents of the Louisiana Territory became loyal and productive American citizens and participated actively against the traditional enemy, England, during the War of 1812. One of the most colorful episodes of the Battle of New Orleans was the part played by the French pirate Jean Laffite.

Although there was no love lost at the official level between the young Republic and the monarchic French *régimes* of the early nineteenth century, the French *émigrés* of the 1790s had left their imprint on the cultural front. For instance, Brillat-Savarin, the famous author of the *Physiology of Taste*, who traveled to the United States where he became extremely fond of American turkey, brought to the New World some of its culinary vocabulary, including the words *menu* and *demitasse*. French books and objects of art were imported by well-to-do Americans. French chefs, French professors, French fencing masters were greatly sought after. During the whole course of the nineteenth century, the American *élite* continued to appreciate a certain image of France. Henry Adams' *Mont Saint-Michel and Chartres* admiringly presented those great Gothic monuments to a highly receptive audience. Women especially were enamored of all things French.

On the eve of the First World War, Americans loved French culture, and paid little attention to French politics. On the other hand, the French were much intrigued by the Far West and by the workings of the American democracy, which had been praised and analyzed in detail by essayist Alexis de Tocqueville in his famous book, *La Démocratie en Amérique* (*Democracy in America*).

The intervention of the United States in the European conflict was probably decisive, and the French were grateful. America was never more popular in France than in 1917–18.

Mont St.-Michel. *French Embassy*

Ironically, however, with the advent of peace, the situation deteriorated. The negotiations which followed the Armistice created misunderstandings. There was a strong clash of personalities between Clemenceau and Wilson, even though the former spoke English well, had spent two years in America, and even married an American *belle*, whom, it is true, he soon divorced for incompatibility.

Then there was the question of war debts. The French considered these part of a settlement which made them contingent on the payment of "reparations" by Germany.

The Germans ceased to pay at the time of the Great Depression and therefore the French also stopped their payments. Opinion in the United States proceeded to stigmatize France for this, despite the fact that most of America's former Allies, sooner or later, also reneged on their debts.

During the twenties, however, many American intellectuals and artists, like Gertrude Stein, Ernest Hemingway, Henry Miller, Anaïs Nin, Julian Green, and many others, went to France to live and write. "Paris was my mistress," wrote one of those expatriates on the title page of a book of memoirs he devoted to this period. The French capital seemed to them a refuge against the prevailing mercantilism, against the mediocrity of the "Babbitt" era.

At the same time the French discovered and enjoyed American "jazz," Negro spirituals, and American movies. They were enthusiastic fans of motion picture actors and directors, Charlie Chaplin, Douglas Fairbanks, Mary Pickford, Lillian and Dorothy Gish, William S. Hart, Cecil B. De Mille, etc. They greeted with boundless admiration the works of such writers as Sinclair Lewis, John Dos Passos, Sherwood Anderson, Eugene O'Neill, and William Faulkner, and many French authors were clearly influenced by their American colleagues.

The Second World War, even more than the First, was marked by strong emotional outbursts, and by unpleasant incidents. Again there was a clash of personalities between two statesmen, Franklin Delano Roosevelt and Charles de Gaulle. The United States Government neither liked nor understood General de Gaulle, snubbed him repeatedly, and threatened to give back to Vichy the islands of Saint-Pierre and Miquelon which had been liberated by the "Free French." There were even cases when the police of American cities co-operated with an anti-Gaullist faction by arresting as deserters French sailors who had joined Free French units. American officials vexed the Gaullist followers by referring to them as the "so-called Free French," by organizing an American Military Government for France (A.M.G.O.T.) and by excluding De Gaulle from most of the military and diplomatic plans of the Allies until the end of 1944.

The French people were, once more, grateful for American help and fully appreciated the Marshall Plan. They still liked Americans, and Americans still liked the French, but their governments seemed unable to communicate. France wanted to be treated as one of the Big Four and to be consulted before great decisions were made; the United States, however, thought that France, ruined by the war, had become a negligible quantity on the world chessboard.

Commercial ties between the two countries were not affected by these difficulties. France imported American machinery, chemicals, aircraft parts; it exported, and still exports, to the United States, wines, cheese, art objects, books, as well as many manufactured goods, leather and wood articles, clothing and shoes.

Stronger than the business relations, however, were the cultural ties. The Alliance Française, for instance, may not be as active as the English-speaking Union, but it is still a powerful though loose organization, which can be found in most of the American cities. French is the most popular language, if not in American secondary schools, where French is a close second to Spanish, at least in colleges and universities. French artists and writers are still much in demand.

On the French side, American writers are also much appreciated. Some, like James Jones and Mary McCarthy, have chosen to live in France. Even more important, we may notice the extraordinary development of American studies in colleges and universities, the great interest for American movies, theater, and art, the almost unanimous admiration for scientific and technologic United States accomplishments. When the American astronauts Armstrong and Aldrin landed on the moon, it was almost 4 A.M. in France, but so great was the number of people who spent the night at their television sets that special measures had to be taken to ensure an adequate supply of electricity! The American civilization and way of life are much discussed and envied. Western-style ranches and indeed replicas of western cities are to be found in France and the western type of riding now vies on French soil with the more traditional European styles. As a kind of official acknowledgment that America and its influence are realities to be reckoned with, about every year or so, a best seller explains to the French the achievements of America, the American "know-how," as did the successful *American Challenge*.

Some Frenchmen are afraid that their country will become completely "Americanized," but many feel that the only way it can be a strong survivor in the world of tomorrow is perhaps by following the example of the country of Apollo XI.

IX
France in the World

Until 1939, French schoolchildren used to learn that France, a modest country of 40 million inhabitants, was also a great empire, twenty-five times as large as the "hexagon" and populated by more than 100,000,000 French-speaking individuals. The French Empire is now a thing of the past, and most of the former colonies are now independent, but French influence is still felt in many parts of the world. *Co-operation* has been substituted for *colonialism*, and new relationships have been created, which may be as strong and more durable than the ties that held together the former *Empire Colonial*.

The history of French colonization, however, is part of French history, and the French, who are very conscious of their past and very much attached to the glories of yesteryear, remember with pride the names of great colonial conquerors, builders, and administrators, men like Faidherbe, Savorgnan de Brazza, Galliéni, and Lyautey, whose names are associated with the development of Senegal, the Congo, Madagascar, and Morocco, respectively.

France acquired its colonies during the course of two different periods of time. Besides Canada and India, which they lost to England in 1763, and Louisiana, which they sold to the United States in 1803, the French, under the Old Regime, settled tropical islands such as Guadeloupe and Martinique in the West Indies and Reunion in the Indian Ocean. Haïti, too, was French until the end of the eighteenth century. Guadeloupe, Martinique, and Reunion were the "spice islands" from which ships brought back coffee, cocoa, cane sugar, pepper, and vanilla. These islands, as well as French Guyana, are still overseas *départements*, directly administered by Paris.

The second wave of colonial conquests took place during the nineteenth century. It was directed mostly toward Africa and Indochina. At the beginning of the twentieth century, France held Morocco, Tunisia, Cambodia, and Laos as protectorates. Its colonies comprised most of West Africa, whereas Algeria, conquered and occupied between 1830 and 1848, made up three French *départements* (administrative subdivisions) inhabited by one million and a half French citizens and ten million Arabs.

All those territories were emancipated after the Second World War, some after negotiations, some as a result of a vote, some, like Indochina and Algeria, after long painful conflicts.

Today, there are less Frenchmen abroad than there used to be. A great many former residents of French Indochina, as well as most of the Algerian colonists, known as *pieds noirs* (black feet), many of whom, like their parents, had been born in Africa and had never been to Europe, have been resettled in Metropolitan France. Approximately two million Frenchmen, however, still live outside of France and by their activities contribute to French influence abroad.

An increasingly important governmental agency, that

of the "Co-operation," furnishes administrators, agrono-
mists, technicians, and teachers to most of the new nations and developing countries. Every year since 1965,
France has sent several thousand young men to a kind of
Peace Corps which it recognizes as a substitute for military service. For example, a young, good-looking writer,
winner of the Théophraste Renaudot prize for 1963, Jean-
Marie Le Clezio, was sent to Bangkok to teach literature
for a year in a girls' high school. Other recruits work as
engineers, physicians, architects, etc.

Generally speaking, France devotes more of its gross
national product and national income than any other nation to public and private foreign aid. French enterprise
has quite a remarkable record in foreign lands; it invests
money and helps with construction and the production of
goods necessary to the economies of those countries.

It may be that France's geographical position and large
areas of coastline are responsible for its constant habit of
looking out toward the rest of the world and exporting its
language, culture, and science. Its influence has been
strongly felt throughout history not only in the territories
it governed or colonized, but all over the world. Spe-
cialists, architects, technicians, and engineers range far
and wide, and are still very much in demand in other
countries. We might mention here that the Suez Canal
was built by a Frenchman, Ferdinand de Lesseps. The
city of Washington was designed by Major Lenfant,
another Frenchman: like Paris, the American capital has
large avenues radiating from traffic circles like the spokes
of a wheel. More recently, the Montreal subway, as well
as many dams, railroads, factories, and airports in Asia

and Africa, were built by Frenchmen. Recently, the Rohr
Corporation, builder of aerospace equipment and of the
subway cars for the future San Francisco Bay Area Rapid
Transit system, entered into an agreement with Société de
l'Aérotrain for the manufacture and marketing of the
French firm's high-speed, tracked, air-cushion vehicle systems based on the *Aérotrain* for intra- and interurban as
well as airport access and short-range transport in the
United States and Mexico. The French architect Le Corbusier, who exercised an immense influence on building
styles in North and South America, realized the city of his
dreams at Chandigarh, in India. Henri Chomette designed
the plans for the opera of Addis-Ababa. Vago, Beaudoin,
and Lopez were "maîtres d'oeuvre" (master builders) for
the Hansaviertel in Berlin.

Sometimes French techniques which are neglected in
France are exported abroad where they enjoy an immense
success. For instance, French scientists and engineers have
found ways of improving the construction of prefabri-
cated buildings, using steel, aluminum, and plastics;
and they export their discoveries in this domain to the
Soviet Union and even to the United States. For themselves, however, they prefer traditional building materials and concrete, because they are sentimentally attached to the stone or whatever reminds them of the past.

The French language, as far back as the twelfth century,
was the language of the elites. Marco Polo used French
when he wrote the account of his travels; Leibnitz, Gib-
bon, and many others also wrote in French. French was
the language of diplomacy and the only accepted lan-

High-speed aerotrain. *French Embassy*

guage at the courts of Russia and Sweden. It is still a
major vehicle of French influence in the modern world. It
is the official or working language of many countries: of
the Ivory Coast, Mali, Senegal, etc., in Africa; of Cambodia and Laos in Asia; of Lebanon and Syria in the Middle East; of regions or countries of the Western Hemi-
sphere, such as Quebec and Haïti. More than 500,000
Americans in Louisiana and about the same number in
New England speak some form of French. Thirty-six out
of one hundred and fifteen national delegations at the
United Nations use French as an instrument of international communication. At a recent *Congrès de la Franco-
phonie* (Congress of French-speaking nations), which took
place in Quebec, thirty countries were represented, includ-

ing Algeria, Morocco, Tunisia, Laos, Cambodia, Syria, Lebanon, Madagascar, Switzerland, Belgium, Mauritania and, of course, France and Canada. Most of those countries had, significantly, sent large delegations headed by officials of the highest ranks.

French books, films, and records are imported by all countries, and there are French schools all over the world. More than fifteen hundred *écoles françaises* (French schools) abroad teach a million and a half foreign students. French *lycées* exist in one hundred and thirty-one countries, among them Afghanistan, Algeria, Argentina, Bulgaria, Cambodia, Egypt, Ethiopia, Sweden, Venezuela, Vietnam, the United Kingdom, and the United States. They have approximately 100,000 students of secondary school age. The *Alliance Française* organizes lectures, conferences, exhibits, and many other forms of cultural activity in almost every country. The *Comédie Française*, as well as other prestigious French theater companies, is frequently invited to foreign countries. There are French Institutes of Art and Architecture in Rome, Athens, and Damascus.

It is still possible to speak of *le rayonnement français* or the "radiation" of France, an expression which is difficult to translate adequately, because it is an influence made up of *impondérables,* that is of intangible cultural values. It may be because many countries have recognized this *rayonnement,* that the U.N.E.S.C.O. headquarters were established in Paris.

PIERRE BRODIN, the distinguished French author-critic-educator, has published some dozen books on literature and history. A native of Paris, France, he attended the University of Paris and Harvard University. He has taught French language and literature at Columbia University, McGill University, Mills College, Middlebury College, and Hunter College. He is a regular contributor to various journals on both sides of the Atlantic. For his contributions to education and literature, he has received, among other decorations, the *Chevalier de la Légion d'Honneur*, the *Officier de l'Ordre de Léopold*, and the *Officier des Palmes Académiques*. Mr. Brodin lives in New York City, where he is Director of Studies at the Lycée Français de New York and Dean of the Faculty of Letters at the French University of New York.